09759

BIRDS OF THE WORLD
SONGBIRDS

BIRDS OF THE WORLD
SONGBIRDS

JOHN P.S. MACKENZIE

KEY PORTER BOOKS

Canadian Cataloguing in Publication Data

Mackenzie, John P. S.
　Songbirds

(Birds of the world)
ISBN 1-55013-221-0

1. Thrushes — Pictorial works.　2. Finches—
Pictorial works.　3. Sylviidae — Pictorial works.
4. Wood warblers — Pictorial works.　I. Title.
II. Series: Mackenzie, John P. S.　Birds of the world.

QL674.M24 1990　　598.8′022′2　　C90-093779-3

Design: First Image
Typesetting: First Image
Printed and bound in Italy

Key Porter Books Limited
70 The Esplanade
Toronto, Ontario
Canada M5E 1R2

90 91 92 93 5 4 3 2 1

Page 2: Hooded Warbler (*Wilsonia citrina*)　Although Hooded Warblers prefer swamps and wet woods for nesting in eastern North America, they can also be found in dry habitat in their wintering range from Mexico to Panama. Hooded Warblers nest close to the ground in small bushes and saplings.

Pages 4-5: Evening Grosbeak (*Coccothraustes vespertinus*)　Grosbeaks congregate in flocks, often numbering in the hundreds, feeding noisily, competitively and aggressively, often driving other birds away.

CONTENTS

INTRODUCTION

Left: Kentucky Warbler (*Opornis formosus*)   In the nineteenth century, ornithologist Alexander Wilson gave the Kentucky Warbler its name because that was where it was first found. Kentucky is indeed the center of its breeding range, which includes all of the southeast except Florida. This bird is a female and lacks the sideburns of the male.

Northern Cardinal (*Cardinalis cardinalis*)   The male cardinal's red mantle is named for the color of the church dignitary's robe. The all-red body and the black face are unmistakable at any time of the year. Although it is an increasingly urban bird, its natural habitat includes thickets, forest edges and swamps.

It is a common misunderstanding that birds sing to express joy and that they greet the dawn with their jubilant cries. It is true that the sounds some birds make are more attractive to humans than those of others and, as a consequence, they are thought to sing. In fact, almost every bird makes sounds of some kind, but not all are songbirds. A thrush may produce a series of melodious notes in a pattern that make a song, while a crow, jay or goose may make squawks and rattles that have little appeal to the human ear. In order to distinguish them from other birds that vocalize, songbirds are defined as those with the greatest number of muscles which enable them to make long and complex vocalizations. Ornithologists define these as songs, as opposed to shorter and less complex calls.

Birds make noises in order to communicate, usually with their own young, their mates or with others of the same species, but also with birds of other species and mammals. The most common purpose of communication during the nesting season is to announce to birds of the same species that the singer has established and will defend its own territory. In the case of communal nesters such as murres, this territory may be only a foot or two on a narrow ledge or, in the case of the Whooping Crane, about one square mile. Whatever the range of the defended territory, the holder of the real estate stakes out and maintains its claim principally by singing. This challenge is heard and usually respected by members of the same species. Mammals often achieve the same result by touring the limits of their territories, leaving scent traces as they go.

Another purpose of bird sound is to announce alarm to its mate. In North America everyone has heard the alarm note of the Robin, somewhat harsh and urgent as it flies off. Alarm notes are very pronounced when there is a threat to eggs or young at the nest. Shrill notes are accompanied by nervous movement in the vicinity of the nest and often feints and dives on the intruder. More gentle bird sound is used in attending dependent young that have left the nest. The purpose in this case is to lead them in search of food and to keep them close to the parent.

Birds feeding or flying in flocks have yet another series of noises to communicate, especially among songbirds migrating at night. One can often hear the sibilant notes keeping the flock together as the birds pass overhead.

The song of any species of birds has characteristics that are usually distinct from the songs of other species within a geographical area, although those of different species are sometimes remarkably similar. Within a species individuals may differ slightly in cadence or pitch, just as humans do. More significant differences in song occur in different parts of a species' range. For example, the Yellow Warbler of North and South America has a wide variation of song in its enormous range — a variation that has been captured in recordings. Despite these variations an acute listener would be able to tell that the songs come from birds of the same species.

Bird song can be communicated to humans in a number of ways besides recordings. Roger Tory Peterson, often called the father of North American bird-watching, did this with great effect in his first field guide published in 1934 by using words or groups of words that have the same cadence as a song. Most books follow this pattern. Other authors of books on bird identification use a number of techniques to visually describe song. In 1935 Aretas A. Saunders published *A Guide to Bird Songs* in which he used verbal descriptions together with diagrammatic bars of varying length — straight, ascending, descending, curved and squiggly — all to great effect. Later authors used tiny spectrograms taken from mechanical recording instruments. Early efforts to translate bird song included the use of musical notation, but this required much space on the page and needed a considerable knowledge of music to be useful.

The range of pitch in bird vocalization is enormous, although the songs of songbirds are usually in the higher register. Among those with a low pitch is the American Bittern whose distinctive song is a throaty *oonk-a-lunk* like the baritone of a bullfrog. In the middle range are the thrushes with their flutelike calls, and in the upper end are the finches and warblers. The average pitch of North American warblers is 5,400 hertz compared to the highest note on a piano which is 4,000 hertz. Some of the small songbirds reach a pitch of 7,000 hertz or more. Many people, even those with good hearing, are unable to hear sound above 4,000 hertz, a failing that increases with age. Even those with the most acute hearing are unable to detect the changes in pitch in these upper ranges as the song tumbles out.

Songs of some birds can be imitated successfully by humans, either by voice or by whistling. I once whistled the call of a Black-bellied Plover in a marsh and a single bird circled for some minutes, finally landing on the stern of the boat in which I was sitting. Similarly Black-capped Chickadees can be attracted by whistling, and in Europe the Cuckoo can be imitated by voice.

Given that almost all birds sing, and that they do so primarily as a form of territorial defense, it should follow that they do so only during the nesting season. This is generally the case, but there are exceptions. Mockingbirds in North America sing throughout the year, while Blue Jays are usually silent when nesting.

Birds communicate in other ways. Nighthawks, Woodcock and Snipe dive toward the female on the ground, making a booming sound with their wing or tail feathers. They pull out of the dive close to their mates. Peregrine Falcons dive at great speed, executing rolls to get the female's attention. Ruffed Grouse "drum" in the spring woods, usually while standing on a fallen trunk. This drumroll is achieved by a furious beating of the wings. Western Grebes display by running along the surface of the water with bodies erect and necks arched forward. Cranes of various species carry out an elaborate dance while bowing in a courtly manner, and peacocks spread their magnificent tails.

Humans and other mammals make sound by forcing air through the larynx which is located near the top of the windpipe. Although birds have a larynx, they do not have vocal chords. Their sounds come from the syrinx which is at the other end of the trachea. The syrinx is enveloped by muscles that control the membranes that make sound. There are two to nine pairs of muscles surrounding the syrinx, depending on the species. It would appear that the tracheal tract acts as a chamber that influences the resonance of the sound. Among the birds that do not have a syrinx are the Turkey Vulture and some storks that are capable only of hissing sounds.

Despite all of the above, most people recognize songbirds as a group of small birds noted, by human standards, as those that are attractive to listen to. They include many of the chickadees, tanagers, blackbirds, larks, wrens and vireos, but particularly the finches, the thrushes, their genetic allies the Old World Warblers, and, to a lesser extent, the New World Warblers. We shall describe the last four in this book.

FINCHES AND BUNTINGS

Painted Bunting (*Passerina ciris*)   The splashes of color make this one of the most striking and beautiful of all birds. It nests in the southeastern United States and Mexico, and winters as far south as Panama.

In most books prepared for bird identification the term "finches" is used to include all of those seed-eating species with stout conical bills. Strictly speaking, finches are members of the family Fringillidae of which there are 153 species divided into three subfamilies. The Fringillidae include such species as the Brambling and Chaffinch of Europe, the European and North American goldfinches, the crossbills, grosbeaks and also the Hawaiian honeycreepers, some of which confuse matters further by having long slender bills curved to extract nectar from flowers. For our purposes we shall include the buntings which have the same physical characteristics.

Buntings are part of a family known as Emberizidae. When settlers arrived in North America they applied English language names to the species that they found, often using names for Emberizidae that are, in fact, finches. Thus many "buntings" are known as sparrows in North America and as finches in the Galapagos. The buntings include the North American sparrows, the longspurs, the cardinals, some grosbeaks, the Dickcissel and the saltators of the tropics.

Strong conical bills are the distinguishing feature for almost all buntings and finches. The skulls are stronger than in most other small birds in order to provide the power needed to remove the coverings from hard seeds which constitute their principal diet. The bills are wonderfully adapted for dealing with the different types of food. Most of the North American sparrows feed on the ground, picking up tiny seeds from the grasses and weeds. Their bills are stubby and conical. The grosbeaks, or in French "gros bec," live up to their name because they have massive bills which they use to pry open large seeds of trees. The Yellow Grosbeak of Mexico has, perhaps, the largest bill of all for it is almost the same size as the rest of the head. Crossbills feed entirely on the seeds of conifers, and live in the northern forests of Europe and North America. The mandibles are sharply pointed at the tip and cross to provide a tool and leverage to open the cones of pine, spruce and other trees for the seeds hidden in the flaps. The nesting season of crossbills is determined by the availability of seeds. When pine and spruce are present, nesting may take place at almost any time of the year. In some parts of northern Europe, where only one kind of tree is available, the seeds may ripen only in winter and the crossbills must nest at temperatures below freezing.

Buntings and finches migrate to or live permanently in almost every part of the world, with the exception of southeast Asia, Australia and New Zealand. Those species that nest in the far north or south migrate in winter to areas where food is available, but many go to areas where harsh climates predominate. The Lapland Longspur and Snow Bunting nest near the shores of the Arctic Ocean, but many remain in winter as far north as grass heads can be seen above the snow.

While buntings and finches may feed almost exclusively on seeds for most of the year, many species feed themselves and their young on insects and grubs during the nesting season when protein requirements are high. Among the migrants the male arrives earlier than the female, often returning to the same place where he bred the previous year. Here he establishes his territory, announcing his presence by song. Some open country species, such as Longspurs and Snow Buntings, sing while flying over their territory, and build their nests on the ground or in a low bush. Woodland and forest-edge species nest in bushes, trees, and on or near the ground.

Bird populations of many species have been known to extend or even contract their ranges over a period of years. Species with long north-south migration passages may be blown into new areas by storms during the spring migration. The case of the Evening Grosbeak is interesting. In a 1946 publication this bird is described as breeding in the north end of its range from Michigan to central British Columbia, and occurring as far east as New England in the winter. During the next few years the breeding territory exploded eastward to the Atlantic provinces of Canada, and the bird became a common winter resident and breeding species in Ontario and Quebec. Similarly the Northern Cardinal, whose northeastern limits were southern Ontario until about 20 years ago, has now expanded northward and at least 1,000 miles further east.

The artificial introduction of species into new areas is seldom successful and is often accompanied by undesirable side effects. For example, the introduction of Starlings and House Sparrows from Europe to North America during the nineteenth century has put pressure on indigenous species through competition for nesting space and food. A happier example was the introduction of House Finches from the southwestern United States into New England during the 1940s. These attractive rosy-colored little birds have added to the charm of southern Canada without apparent harm to other species.

Most people, particularly in North America, think of finches and buntings as a group, and usually dismiss them as "just more of those little brown birds." This is understandable because there are more than 30 species of sparrows in North America that look just like that — little brown birds. Even experienced observers may have trouble identifying sparrows unless they sing. The distinguishing features are often so slight that unless the birds are sitting still in good light, which they seldom do, they cannot be properly identified. Some sparrows have a habit of flying only a short distance when disturbed and then diving into deep grass.

Apart from the sparrows, many of the buntings and finches are wonderfully clothed in yellows, pinks and blues. Usually the males are brighter with more distinct patterns than the females. Juveniles of most species, and the females of many, undoubtedly may be classified as "little brown birds." The most elaborate is the Painted Bunting which lives from the southern United States to Panama. It has unbroken patches of blue, bright green, red and black. Others of note are the Northern Cardinal, the Blue Grosbeak, the Indigo Bunting and the American Goldfinch. In Europe the Bullfinch, with its bright red underparts, and the Goldfinch, with its yellow wing patches and red face, are outstanding. In both Eurasia and America there are a number of finches which are rosy colored or which have dominant red patches. Three of these, the Red Crossbill (known in Europe as the Common Crossbill), the White-winged Crossbill (also known as the Two-barred Crossbill) and the Pine Grosbeak are common to both continents.

Lazuli Bunting (*Passerina amoena*) The male Lazuli Bunting has a brilliant turquoise head and nape. The nest is built in low bushes, usually in deciduous woodlands, close to water.

Evening Grosbeak (*Coccothraustes vespertinus*) This was once a purely
western bird, nesting mainly in the mountains in mixed forest. During the
past 40 or 50 years its range has expanded to the extent that it is now
common in Maritime Canada and New England.

Lazuli Bunting (*Passerina amoena*)   The bird's turquoise and cinnamon coloring can be seen to advantage. This bird nests in southern British Columbia, Alberta and throughout the western United States. It winters in Mexico.

Pine Grosbeak (*Pinicola enucleator*) This is a female or immature male. They nest across northern Europe and from northern Alaska to Newfoundland and as far south as New Mexico, usually in the lower branches of conifers. Food consists of the seeds of conifers, beech and other trees.

Left: Blue Grosbeak (*Guiraca Caerulea*) The Blue Grosbeak has broad chestnut wing bars that distinguish it from the smaller but similarly colored Indigo Bunting. It nests across the United States as far north as New Jersey and as far south as Costa Rica.

Snow Bunting (*Plectrophenax nivalis*)   The black mantle shown here is the summer plumage. In winter this is replaced by a mottled pale brown, so that in flight, a flock of snow buntings appears to be completely white from some angles and brown from others.

Right: Pine Grosbeak (*Pinicola enucleator*)   The male has a reddish head and back and flashing white wing bars. The song varies throughout the bird's wide range, but is a melodious series of warbles, whistles and trills, both loud and soft.

Rose-breasted Grosbeak (*Pheucticus ludovicianus*)   This male, with his massive white bill and rosy chest patch, is feeding young. A North American nester from the northern prairies of Canada to the southeastern United States, it migrates to southern Mexico, Venezuela and Equador in winter. The melodious song is similar to that of the American Robin.

Lapland Longspur (*Calcarius lapponicus*)   This nestling will develop striking markings when it matures. Adult males have a dark head and breast, a white zigzag from face to flank, and a chestnut nape. In Europe it is known as the Lapland Bunting. It is circumpolar, nests on the far northern tundra, and generally moves farther south in winter.

Left: Chestnut-collared Longspur (*Calcarius ornatus*)   During the nesting season, this bird lives in the central prairies of Canada and the United States, where it nests close to moist ground, usually in thick grass. It migrates to the southwestern United States and northern Mexico in winter.

Chestnut-collared Longspur (*Calcarius ornatus*)   This bird is in winter plumage. In summer it is strongly marked about the face, has black underparts and a chestnut-colored patch at the back of the neck. Its song is a fast warble, which is heard during the breeding season from the ground or from the air.

Purple Finch (*Carpodacus purpureus*) This female lacks the rosy coloring of
the male. Originally they nested in clearings in the forests of North America
near streams or swamps. They have taken readily to urban parks and
gardens, using the many plantings of coniferous trees.

OLD WORLD WARBLERS

Ruby-crowned Kinglet (*Regulus calendula*)   This tiny bird has a remarkable song—a number of high-pitched *zees*, followed by lower-pitched *tews*, and then a loud jumble of tinkling melody, all in ascending notes.

Old World Warblers constitute the subfamily of birds known as Sylviinae which is one of 11 subfamilies of the large family of Muscacipidae. Just how may Sylviinae there are depends on the authority used, for there is little agreement among taxonomists as to whether many of the species are, in fact, true warblers. The number varies from 339 to 422. The confusion is illustrated by the admixture in some of the vernacular names, e.g. tit-flycatchers and tit-weavers. Further, the term Old World Warbler is deceptive for 13 species of gnatcatchers and gnatwrens and two species of kinglets live in North and South America.

Members of the subfamily Sylviinae live in all parts of the world except the extreme north and in southern South America. All are small, insect-eating birds found principally in Europe, Africa and Asia where they may be found in almost any habitat from marshes, forests and plains to deserts. Australia has eight to 33 species, while New Zealand has one. Many species exist on only a single island or on a remote mountain in New Guinea or on the Solomon Islands. Some of these isolated native species have only tiny populations whose existence is threatened by natural catastrophe, logging and human sprawl. One species, the Aldabra Warbler, had only 11 known birds in 1983.

Those insect-eating warblers that nest in northern Europe and Asia must migrate to warm climates for the winter, some traveling great distances. The European Willow Warbler migrates from its summer range as far north as the northern tip of Norway to central Africa, a distance of 7,500 miles. In East Africa during the winter it can scarcely be distinguished from its close ally, the resident Brown Woodland Warbler. In order to undertake these prodigious journeys, warblers must increase their food intake, some doubling their weight in fat reserves. Some species remain quite far north in winter, surviving precariously on grubs and insect eggs tucked in the bark of trees. These include the Dartford Warbler, the Blackcap and the Chiffchaff, some of whose members remain in southern England where, in hard winters, many die.

Although there are exceptions, Old World Warblers tend to be rather plain and drab in appearance, paler below than above, in a variety of shades of yellow, dull green, brown and gray. Most have a pale stripe above the eye and thin, pointed bills. Field identification of many species is difficult for several reasons. There are many look-alikes. The differences in color and markings, which are apparent in a well illustrated field guide, disappear during the few seconds that one might catch a glimpse of the bird. Many species are skulkers, particularly the reed warblers that remain low in thick, wet vegetation. Others live in dense tangles and spend most of the time running about on the ground like a mouse. In many cases sound is the only sure way to distinguish one species from another within any range because the songs are distinctive. In Europe the Chiffchaff and the Willow Warbler are indistinguishable by sight, but the songs are entirely different. The former repeats its name while the latter makes a series of descending notes. Song differences help only during the nesting season because that is the only time they sing. Many of these warblers are mimics. The Marsh Warbler, for example, does not have a song of its own, but mimics the songs of nearly 100 species, many of which it learned during the winter in Africa.

Old World Warblers are strongly territorial. Nesting pairs defend an area for feeding against others of their own species and often against members of different species. Different warbler species will, however, often share a territory if they do not compete for the same food. Some prefer small insects, which they take on the wing while hovering among leaves, while others prefer larger insects. Territories vary in size, depending upon the food supply.

We have noted earlier that Australia has a minimum of eight species of Old World Warblers. This number may be increased to 33 if one includes the thornbills, whitefaces and fairy warblers which some authorities do. In Australia the warblers build domed nests. Some are sedentary while others migrate seasonally within the country. The nine species of fairy warblers are more active than the others while foraging in the trees. Other groups remain low or on the ground.

Warblers nest close to the ground, usually in dense thickets or in marshes. Nests are elaborately woven of grasses and may be cup-shaped or domed. Eggs vary in number from two to seven, with incubation taking place in two weeks or slightly less. Young birds mature quickly, leaving the nest about two weeks after hatching. They are dependent on their parents for a time, but during this period the parents may be preparing for another brood.

It has been mentioned that the kinglets of the New World are Old World Warblers. The Firecrest (Regulus Ignicapillus) of Europe and the Golden-crowned Kinglet (Regulus Satrapa) of North America so closely resemble one another that they appear to be indistinguishable. During the winter, the Firecrest stays as far north as southern England, and the Golden-crowned Kinglet as far as the northern United States. The Firecrest and its close relative the Goldcrest are the smallest birds nesting in Europe — only three-and-one-half inches long. In North America the two kinglets are early migrants arriving in the spring, usually weeks before most of the warblers.

In Europe the warblers are divided into groups of allies. The *Locustella* Warblers are dark brown above and pale brown below, all lacking wing bars. The 13 species of Reed Warblers are all fairly dark brown above and rosy beige on the underparts. All but two species have rounded tails. The Graceful and Scrub warblers of southeastern Europe and Africa have long tails which they fan from side to side. The six species of *Hippolais* warblers are uniformly colored from yellow to gray. The Melodious Warbler in this group has a lovely liquid song which it seems to rush through. The 18 species of *Sylvia* Warblers vary considerably in appearance from the nondescript Whitethroats and Garden Warblers to such strongly marked species as the Sardinian, Menetries', Cyprus and Ruppell's warblers. The last group consists of the 11 Leaf warblers which are small greenish birds with some yellow. It includes the very widespread Willow Warbler and the Chiffchaff.

The Garden Warbler makes up in song for what it lacks in appearance. Its throaty warble of rich notes may be heard all over Europe from April until mid-July when it becomes secretive and silent except for the occasional *shack* call. Each bird may sing for as much as half the day during the nesting season. The name Garden Warbler is inappropriate because it nests in the thorny scrub of hedges, thickets at the edge of woods, and in brushy common land. By mid-September this warbler disappears from Europe to winter in central Africa.

A close relative of the Garden Warbler is the Blackcap, appropriately distinguished by its black cap. The cap is reddish brown in the female. This bird winters to some extent in southern England, but most go farther south to the shores of the Mediterranean, arriving back in the nesting areas as early as March. The song consists of prolonged warbling and whistling which start rather quietly and ascend in volume to end in a distinctive whistle, making it even more beautiful than that of the Garden Warbler. It also nests and feeds in scrub and brambles.

The Willow Warbler is the most common of the Sylviidae in Europe. It nests as far as the northern tip of Scandinavia and winters in southern

Europe and Africa. Despite its name, the Willow Warbler is more attracted to hazel, birch and oak than to willows where it will only be seen in any numbers in the early spring. The song of this bird is beautiful — a series of descending notes, unrushed and lilting.

Many Old World Species are sedentary or nomadic, moving about only as food supplies dictate. In Africa and Asia most species have a fairly wide range where they seem to prefer thorn bushes, secondary vegetation and grassland, although some species feed and nest high in the forest canopy.

Ruby-crowned Kinglet (*Regulus calendula*)   The two kinglet species and the
Blue-gray Gnatcatcher of North America are classified as Old World
Warblers. The Ruby-crowned Kinglet nests from Alaska to Newfoundland,
but is only present as a migrant in the central and eastern United States.

Ruby-crowned Kinglet (*Regulus calendula*) The ruby-colored crown, seldom seen from above, is shown. While Ruby-crowned Kinglets usually feed close to the ground, these birds build a round hanging nest high in an evergreen tree in thick cover near the end of a branch.

Left: Golden-crowned Kinglet (*Regulus satrapa*) Nests are built high in spruce or other conifers, and are round with an entrance at the top. It feeds on insects, eggs and larvae. The Golden-crowned Kinglet sings only during the nesting season, and its song is a series of notes followed by a high-pitched, almost inaudible trill.

Golden-crowned Kinglet (*Regulus satrapa*) Closely resembling the related Goldcrests and Firecrests of Europe, the Golden-crowned Kinglet nests as far north as the border of the Northwest Territories. Most of the species withdraw to the southern United States in winter.

White-chinned Prinia (*Prinia leucopogon*) There are 21 species of prinias, most of them in Africa. The White-chinned Prinia lives mostly from the Cameroon to Angola and in Tanzania.

Blue-gray Gnatcatcher
(*Polioptila caerulea*)
Nesting throughout
the southeastern
United States and
wintering as far south
as Guatemala, this
long-tailed bird is an
active feeder on insects
in open woodlands. It
often hovers near the
ends of branches,
snapping insects from
the leaves.

Eastern Crowned Warbler (*Phylloscopus coronatus*) Most of the large *Phylloscopus* group of Old World Warblers live in Asia and the Pacific islands, although some species are widespread in Europe. These leaf warblers are noted for flicking tails and wings. The Eastern Crowned Warbler is widespread in eastern Asia.

Right: Clamorous Reed Warbler (*Acrocephalus stentoreus*) An Old World Warbler that is closely related to the widespread Great Reed Warbler of Europe and Asia, this bird nests around the southeast corner of the Mediterranean. The 13 species of reed warblers found in Europe are disconcertingly similar, almost impossible to identify visually, although their songs are different.

Greenish Leaf Warbler (*Phylloscopus trochiloides*)   The color of this warbler
varies from greenish to grayish-brown. It nests in central and northern
Eurasia and southeast Asia in open woodland and at the edges of forests.

Black-collared Apalis (*Apalis pulchra*)   The *Apalis* group of Old World Warblers have long, narrow tails. The Black-collared Apalis often raises its tail and wags it from side to side. It lives in the highlands of Kenya and Uganda, where it is found in the undergrowth and bushes.

African Reed Warbler
(*Acrocephalus
baeticatus*) Reed
warblers live and nest
in marshes in the
temperate parts of the
Old World. This one
nests from Sudan to
the Cape Province of
South Africa.

Victorin's Scrub Warbler (*Bradypterus victorini*)   There are 18 species of scrub warblers in the genera *Bradypterus,* most of which live in Africa, while others live in Asia, Borneo, Java and the Philippines. The Victorin's Scrub Warbler lives in the mountains of the Cape Province of South Africa.

Blue-gray Gnatcatcher (*Polioptila caerulea*) The Blue-gray Gnatcatcher has
a narrow white eye ring and a black-and-white tail.

Gray-backed Camaroptera (*Camaroptera brevicaudata*) A common resident species from central and eastern Africa to South Africa, the Gray-backed Camaroptera inhabits thick underbrush and bushes in a wide range of habitats from semi-deserts to forests in the mountains. Its call is a long, plaintive *squeee.*

Knysna Scrub Warbler (*Bradypterus sylvaticus*)   This scrub warbler is one of
the African species and lives from Natal to South Africa. The long, flat and
rounded tail is typical of its genera.

NEW WORLD WARBLERS

Chestnut-sided Warbler (*Dendroica pensylvanica*)   The population of this species has increased since the forests of the eastern United States and Canada were cleared. It prefers open, second-growth deciduous woods for nesting and feeding.

The formal classification of animals and plants into families, subfamilies, genera and species dates from the eighteenth century which was a period of geographical and natural exploration. In 1758 the great Swedish naturalist Linnaeus published *Systema Naturae* and introduced internationally accepted names for all known animal species. It became clear with the growth of knowledge that the basis of Linnaeus's work was flawed because he and other naturalists of the period relied on only the skins of birds and other animals to make their classifications, unlike later naturalists who analyzed bones and organs in addition to skins. An important consideration in songbird classification was the number of primary feathers on the wing of a bird. Old World Warblers were known to have ten. The specimens of the bright little birds coming from America, which were not then known as warblers, had nine primary feathers. Other considerations were the shape of the bill, the presence of a crest, the length and shape of the wings and tail, and distinctive patterns and color.

As a result of inaccurate classification, many members of the family of birds now known as Wood Warblers or Parulidae were assigned arbitrarily to several other families. Nineteen species became wagtails, three became thrushes, and five were classified as flycatchers. Not until the early to mid-nineteenth century did Alexander Wilson and John James Audubon describe them as warblers. Later in the nineteenth century, when more advanced work was done, at least three names were assigned to the family before it became Parulidae. This research was based on an analysis of the bones and organs of the birds in addition to the external features seen from the skins alone. Today the Parulidae are recognized as a subfamily of the Emberizidae.

As recently as 1957 it was thought that there were 116 species of Parulidae. By 1985 this number had become 123. In addition to changing classifications the American Ornithologists Union has a habit of changing the English or vernacular names of birds, putting identification books out of date, often before they are available for sale. Since 1957 the Myrtle Warbler and Audubon's warblers combined to become the Yellow-rumped Warbler, the Canada Jay the Gray Jay, the Olive-backed Thrush the Swainson's Thrush, and so on.

The number of warbler species changes because they hybridize, because more bird-watchers are discovering more species, and because the level of anatomical research has led to differing conclusions. The hybridization of the Blue-winged Warbler and the Golden-winged

Warbler produces the Brewster's or Lawrence's warblers. Unlike crosses between horses and donkeys, these warblers are fertile. Many other hybrids have occurred, the Blackpoll and Bay-breasted, the Cape May and Blackpoll, the Audubon's and the Myrtle, for example. It was thought for a time that a new species called Sutton's Warbler had been discovered, but it was later agreed that it was a hybrid of the Parula and the Yellow-throated.

Be that as it may, the New World or Wood Warblers, as they are more properly called, are to me, the most attractive family of birds. Most are brilliantly colored and patterned in yellow, orange, red, black and white. They flit about at all elevations from the treetops to the lower branches, searching the leaves for aphids and other small insects. Some flutter near the ends of the branches or dart out like flycatchers in their constant search for food. Others, such as the Ovenbird and the waterthrushes, spend most of their time on the ground.

Wood Warblers have narrow pointed bills suitable for catching insects. All are small birds varying in length from four-and-a-half inches to seven inches. Not all species are brilliantly colored. Some, such as the Tennessee, the Orange-crowned and Virginia's, are rather dull, somewhat resembling vireos. The difference is that vireos have thicker, stubby bills. Immature and post-molt warblers tend to have the same patterns as do those in spring plumage, but the colors are subdued and often difficult to place.

Parulidae range from Alaska to Argentina. Almost half of the 123 species are found north of Mexico, most only during the nesting season. Some remain in the southwestern or southeastern parts of the United States during the winter, while a few hardier species, such as the Yellow-rumped, remain in the east, subsisting on berries. Most of the northern nesting species abandon North America in the autumn to winter in the West Indies, Cuba, Central and South America. Few migrants move south of the Equator.

Warblers move about in loose flocks in the tropics. It is often easier to find large numbers of warblers in their southern winter range than it is in the north where, after the wave of migration, they become dispersed through the vast forests.

Both northern and southern migration take place in easy stages. In late winter those from South and Central America start north, moving gradually with the weather. They reach the northeastern states and southern Canada toward the end of April and reach the peak in numbers in mid-May. The Black-and-White Warbler is usually among the first to arrive. It can find insect eggs from the previous year as it scours the bark on trunks and branches of trees. In southern Ontario large numbers of people flock to Point Pelee on Lake Erie where, apart from seeing about 35 species of warblers in a day, they can reasonably expect a count of 100 others. The Blackpoll Warbler is one of the last to arrive, not becoming common until after the bird-watchers have left.

The family of Parulidae is the most abundant group of birds in eastern North America. Being forest dwellers only a few, such as the Yellow Warbler, are seen in gardens except during migration. During the nesting season they establish territories, mostly in spruce and pine forests, but some, like the Black-throated Blue Warbler, prefer upland mixed or deciduous woods and usually nest on well-drained hillsides. Habitat extends from the ground to the treetops, making it practical for several species to share the same territory without competing for food or nesting space. The Mourning Warbler and the Ovenbird scavenge on the ground. The Mourning Warbler also, like the Wilson's and the Swainson's, lives in the underbrush. The Chestnut-sided and Yellow warblers forage in mid-elevations. Others, including the Blackburnian and Black-throated Green warblers feed and nest high in the trees.

Large numbers of warbler species are sedentary or migratory within only a relatively small area in the south. Some 23 species exist solely in Central America or range from there into South America. An additional 25 species are found only in South America, and 16 only in the West Indies and Cuba. Several of these live only on one island or on one mountainside where they are, as a species, exposed to the dangers of a limited range.

The huge numbers of northern nesting birds that migrate to Central and South America rely on the food to be found in the forests there. In northern Central America and Mexico, where forests are being destroyed much faster than they can regenerate, suitable winter habitat is being reduced at an alarming rate. Many observers have noted that they see fewer and fewer warblers each year, blaming the decline on the loss of winter habitat.

Long migrations add to the hazards facing small birds. Great numbers, attracted to the strong light, smash into lighthouses at night. Tall buildings which remain lit at night are another fatal attraction, their bases surrounded in the morning by dead and dying birds. Storms and cold weather kill great numbers of insect-eating birds that may, after an overnight flight, find that there are no insects to eat. They then weaken so that they become unable to forage. Small birds have a short life expectancy. One Black-and-White Warbler is known to have lived for 11 years, but few survive long enough to nest more than once.

There is no such thing as a typical warbler song nor, to my ear, do many of them warble. Most have reasonably recognizable songs which, as mentioned in the Introduction, vary considerably in different nesting areas of their range and even between individuals in the same area. Although their songs are pleasant, they are not particularly good singers as a group. They make weak hissing sounds of rattles and trills. The Yellow-breasted Chat, the largest of the Parulidae, makes a series of squawks and slurring whistles. The songs of most warblers can be heard for some distance in the quiet forest. Many of the songs are very high on the scale, some twice as high as the top note of a piano.

When northern nesting warblers are in their winter habitat in the tropics, they do not sing at all. By the time they reach the southern United States they start to sing, sometimes half-formed songs. Toward the end of their migration they are singing freely, but at a time when the woods are ringing with the sound of thrushes, finches and sparrows, one must be quite close to the warblers in order to distinguish their songs from those of the rest. In the nesting area they sing almost constantly in defense of their territory until the young have left the nest. They then sing less frequently, usually in a rather bored manner.

Because of their cheerful character the songs of some warblers can be represented quite effectively by words on the page, rather more so than with the songs of other families of songbirds. Most people are familiar with the Yellow Warbler which is common in gardens and in the wild during the summer all over North America as far north as there are bushes. One writer has described its song as *sweet sweet sweet I'm so sweet*, and another as *tzee tzee tzee tzee tsitta tsitta tsee*. However one interprets each sound, it can readily be seen from these two descriptions that the songs vary greatly, and the best that can be achieved through words is to express a series of symbols to aid the memory. Similarly the song of the Black-throated Blue Warbler may be described as *zee-oo zee-oo-zee* or, alternately, *I am so la-zee*.

Prairie Warbler (*Dendroica discolor*)   An eastern species, the Prairie Warbler prefers abandoned fields, scrub and open forest. Its name is misleading because it nests in bushes or in mangroves overlooking water. Its song is a series of ascending *zee, zee, zees*.

American Redstart (*Setophaga ruticilla*)   The American Redstart has been described as "the candle of the forest." The male is a handsome black and orange, and its fluttering among coniferous trees can be likened to a flickering candle.

Left: Black-and-white Warbler (*Mniotilta varia*) Widespread from eastern North America to the Northwest Territories, the Black-and-white Warbler behaves more like a nuthatch—it forages along branches for hidden insects. Like most warblers, it does not warble but utters a series of two-note phrases.

Yellow-rumped Warbler (*Dendroica coronata*) This is a female Yellow-rumped Warbler, formerly known as Audubon's Warbler. The male western Yellow-rumped Warbler has a yellow throat, while its eastern equivalent has a white throat.

Black-throated Green Warbler (*Dendroica virens*)   Nesting from the Appalachians to the Northwest Territories, this attractive warbler prefers remote mixed forests, where it is usually seen high in the trees. Its song is not a warble but a lisping *see, see, see, so, see.*

Right: Yellow-rumped Warbler (*Dendroica coronata*)   Also known as the Myrtle Warbler, this bird's song is sometimes a warble, rather slow and trilling, descending in pitch toward the end.

Golden-winged Warbler (*Vermivora chrysoptera*)   This is a fine example of a
male in courtship plumage. It nests in the eastern United States and
southern Ontario. Hybrids of golden-winged and Blue-winged Warblers can
result in the dissimilar Brewster's and Lawrence's Warblers.

Magnolia Warbler (*Dendroica magnolia*)   The name has little to do with magnolias, except in the southern end of the bird's nesting range, which extends from North Carolina to northern Canada. It nests a few feet from the ground in small conifers.

Left: Ovenbird (*Seiurus aurocapillus*) This bird builds its oven-shaped nest on the ground, usually in a slight hollow. Its song is a strident *teacher, teacher, teacher*. It feeds on insects, snails and grubs, which it turns up while walking on the forest floor.

Yellow Warbler (*Dendroica petechia*) The most wide-ranging North American warbler, the Yellow Warbler nests throughout almost the entire continent and south to Peru. The male has orange stripes on its breast. A southern variant, known as the Mangrove Warbler, has a chocolate-brown head.

Brown-headed Cowbird (*Molothrus ater*)   The cowbird is a blackbird. The
female lays its eggs in the nests of warblers, sparrows and other small birds.
The young cowbirds almost invariably displace the resident young and are
reared by their hosts.

Orange-crowned Warbler (*Vermivora celata*)   This is the drabbest of all the wood warblers, scarcely distinguishable from immature birds and females of other species. It is primarily a western species, but passes through the east during its migration to northern Canada.

Prothonotary Warbler (*Protonotaria citrea*)   Seen here at a nesting hole, this
beautiful warbler creates a flash of gold as it flies through the forest. It has a
ringing *tweet, tweet, tweet* song. It is not often successful in nesting in the
northern end of its range in Michigan.

Mourning Warbler (*Oporornis philadelphia*) The Mourning Warbler is similar to the Connecticut and MacGillivray's Warblers, although it lacks the white eye ring. During the summer it is found in the dense undergrowth of moist woods from the northeastern United States to northern Canada. It winters in Central and South America.

Left: Yellow-breasted Chat (*Icteria virens*)   At seven inches, this is the largest of the wood warblers. The Yellow-breasted Chat is a reclusive bird that nests in dense tangles of vines and in thickets. It lives throughout the United States and occurs sparsely in southern Canada. The male will hop up to sing from a perch or while hovering near the nest.

Palm Warbler (*Dendroica palmarum*)   The principal identifying mark is the brown cap on this otherwise plain bird, which nests eastward from Alberta, as well as in the northern United States. In winter, Palm Warblers migrate to Florida and the Gulf Coast where they forage on or close to the ground.

Wilson's Warbler (*Wilsonia pusilla*) Named for the ornithologist Alexander Wilson, it is a northern and western species that spends the summer from Alaska to Newfoundland. It forages for insects on the ground where it also nests, usually at the base of a small tree.

Bay-breasted Warbler (*Dendroica castanea*) This is a female on the nest. The male is strikingly patterned in black and rich brown. It nests in coniferous forests across central Canada and the United States.

Black-throated Blue Warbler (*Dendroica caerulescens*) This female has nested in an evergreen. Black-throated Blue Warblers usually nest in birch and other deciduous trees at mid-elevation. It has a characteristic white fleck on its wing.

Yellow-rumped Warbler (*Dendroica coronata*) This western specimen used to be known as the Audubon's Warbler. The yellow throat distinguishes it from its eastern counterpart, with which it hybridizes in overlapping ranges.

MacGillivray's Warbler (*Oporonis tolmiei*) Similar to the Mourning Warbler and to the Connecticut, the MacGillivray's Warbler breeds in the western United States and British Columbia. It migrates to Mexico and Guatemala. It builds its nest close to the ground in brush or tall weeds and ferns.

Kentucky Warbler (*Oporonis formosus*) In 1912, ornithologist Frank
Chapman counted the number of times the Kentucky Warbler sang. In three
hours, the bird sang 875 times. It nests and forages on the ground, and is
often hard to find even after the song is heard.

Black-throated Blue Warbler (*Dendroica caerulescens*)   This male is unmistakable in its neat plumage of blue, black and white. It nests from Manitoba to Nova Scotia and south through the mountains to South Carolina. It migrates to the West Indies and Columbia.

Yellow-rumped Warbler (*Dendroica coronata*) Even in winter plumage the Yellow-rumped is distinguishable by the bright yellow patch at the base of its tail. It is found across the United States, where this hardy bird remains throughout the year. It nests all over North America, except on the prairies, and as far north as Alaska.

Right: Nashville Warbler (*Vermivora ruficapilla*) The prominent white eye ring is the distinguishing feature of the Nashville Warbler. It is found in second-growth bush of mixed young trees or boggy forests in the north. It nests on the ground across Canada south of Hudson Bay and in the northeastern United States. There is a separate population in the Northwest.

Northern Waterthrush (*Seiurus noveboracensis*) The Northern and Louisiana Waterthrushes differ slightly in appearance. The eyestripe of the former is narrower, more buff in color, and does not extend as far back. It also has less color on the flanks and belly.

Northern Waterthrush (*Seiurus noveboracensis*)   The nest is built on the ground, usually in the roots of fallen trees or in tree stump cavities. It feeds on the ground close to or along the edge of ponds and streams.

Louisiana Waterthrush (*Seiurus motacilla*)   The Louisiana Waterthrush lives in wet areas of the eastern United States and southern Canada. Note that the eye stripe extends to the nape.

Stonechat (*Saxicola torquata*) This bird is a female. The male has a black head with a white ring that extends to the nape. It is a year-round resident of the British Isles and southern Europe. Northern European and Asian birds move south in winter. The Stonechat nests on moors, cliffs, alpine country, and on farms.

Short-toed Rock Thrush (*Monticola brevipes*)   This elegant little thrush, with its red underparts and prominent white eye stripe, is found only at the southern tip of Africa.

Chorister Robin Chat (*Cossypha dichroa*)   A handsome tricolored thrush in gold, blue and black, the Chorister Robin Chat is a resident species in southern Africa from Natal to South Africa.

Right: European Rock Thrush (*Monticola saxatilis*)   A summer resident of southern Europe and Asia Minor, it withdraws to Africa and Asia in winter. It is a mountain bird, more often heard than seen, and has a lovely piping song. It is usually a solitary bird, but sometimes forms loose flocks when migrating.

Rufous Rock Jumper (*Chaetops frenatus*)   This handsome thrush is endemic to the southwestern Cape Province of South Africa, and lives at elevations above 2,000 feet. It seldom flies, preferring to jump from rock to rock, or to run on the few flat places in its rough habitat.

Ground-scraper Thrush (*Zoothera Listipsirupa*)   The Ground-scraper Thrush
is a fairly large thrush measuring approximately nine inches. It is a fairly
common resident species from the highlands of Ethiopia and through
central Africa to South Africa. It has a loud, clear song of repeated liquid
whistles. Orange wing patches are prominent when the bird flies.

European Blackbird (*Turdus merula*) Probably the most numerous of all European birds, this bird is found throughout the year in all but Scandinavia and northern Russia. Some birds winter in north Africa. The female is dark brown with the streaked breast common to many thrushes. It lives in forests of all kinds and is common in urban areas.

White-starred Bush Robin (*Pogonocichla stellata*)   A resident bird in East Africa, the Congo and South Africa, this robin-like bird lives in the forest where it prefers extensive bamboo patches. It feeds mostly on the ground, feasting on safari ants.